D0103795

Seeking the Tresures of The Quran

Dr. Mazhar U. Kazi

Al-Huda Publications

Copyright © 2005 by
Al-Huda Publications

Third Revised Edition: **Jan 2006**

ISBN 0-9763450-2-1

Manufactured in the United States
Al-Huda Publications

400 Industrial Drive, Suite 100
Richardson, TX 75081

Website: www.alhudapublishers.com

With the name of Allah, the Most Compassionate, the Most Merciful

CONTENTS

FOREWORD

All praises and thanks are to Allah, the One, the Supreme, the Most Compassionate, the Most Merciful and the Most Forgiving. There is no strength to do any good or to avoid any evil except through His Grace and Mercy.

Allah's Peace and Blessings be upon His blessed Prophet Muhammad, the last of Allah's Messengers, the seal of the chain of prophets, the mercy to mankind, the illuminating light, and my intercessor on the Day of Judgment. Allah's Peace and Blessings be upon his family, his companions and all those who follow him on the right path.

Books represent a method of conveying ideas and knowledge from person to person and from place to place. To this end, all books share some common characteristics. All books, whether existing or extinct, were written by human beings. All books relate to a certain domain of human knowledge and have a common format. All books are divided into chapters, each chapter addresses a specific topic, and each topic presents the text in a defined sequence.

When evaluated in light of the above-mentioned criteria of the worldly books, the Quran is not like a worldly book. It has its own unique features, not shared by any worldly book. It was not written by a human being, it does not relate exclusively to issues encompassed by human knowledge and experiences. Its discourse, format and style are unmatched and unique. The central theme of the Quran is faith. Its specific subject is the relationship of faith to humanity. The reader, at the very start, should accept these unique features of the Quran, and should not compare it with a worldly book.

In this regard a prudent reader must observe that, although current literature is rife with abundant supply of other books of faith, original manuscripts of all of those books are either lost or they have been contaminated with human expressions to a greater or lesser extent. On the other hand, The Quran is the only existing book of faith, which has always remained, categorically and absolutely, pure and unadulterated, in its original form. This is a historical fact, which has always remained a universal truth, beyond even a flickering shadow of doubt or contention. Thus, Quran has been and will always remain the most unique and the only original and pure book of its kind.

In this booklet, "Seeking Treasures of The Quran", I have made a humble attempt to explain a few unique features of the Quran. It is my earnest hope that the reader will not only begin to appreciate the beauties of this Blessed Revelations, but will also grasp some of its miraculous marvels and wonders. At the same time, this would hopefully help the readers to benefit from the boundless treasures of wisdom and blessings of this Blessed Revelation.

This book has been published earlier in USA, under the title of "Towards Understanding the Quran" by Al-Huda Publications of Dallas, Texas and Al-Minar Publishers of Philadelphia, Pennsylvania. Also in India, Markazi Maktaba Islami, Delhi, published the same book under the title of "Introduction to the Quran". Ferozesons Ltd (Pakistan) has now published this book from Lahore, and Karachi, entitled as "A guide to understanding the Quran". It was published again in May 2005, by Al-Huda Publications of Dallas Texas, as "Seeking the Treasures of The Quran". The present publication is the third revised version of the same manuscript.

Based on the Hadith "He, who fails to thank his fellow beings, fails to thank Allah" I consider it my duty to thank those persons who helped me in the preparations of this book.

Three persons worked with me closely during the preparation of the first edition of this book; my Sunday Islamic class student, Dr. Carol Etzel of the University of Texas at Houston; Dr. Aarifeen Lodhi of Texas Tech University at Lubbock and Shahid Kamal Pasha, the renowned writer and journalist from Pakistan. May Allah SWT accept their efforts.

The second edition was thoroughly revised with the help of four persons; my Sunday Islamic class student Ms. Samaria Elia, a professional journalist, Mr. A. Hakym, a professional writer, and two academicians, namely Dr. Basheer Khumawala and Dr. Saleha Khumawala of University of Houston. May Allah bless them for their efforts.

The third edition was revised word by word by a very noble friend of mine. He offered himself to undertake this task and has asked me not to mention his name. Allah knows his name and his intention and will hopefully reward him immensely.

I earnestly pray that Allah, the Exalted may accept my humble efforts and make it a means for spreading a better understanding of His Divine Message. I also pray that Allah, the Exalted help others and myself to receive the countless Blessings of the Quran. Amen!

Dr. Mazhar Kazi
Houston, Texas

Zul-Hijjah 1426 AH / Jan 2006 CE

Chapter One

RELIABILITY OF THE QURAN

Allah, the Exalted, has revealed the Quran, to Prophet Muhammad, Peace and Blessings be upon him (PBUH), as final and complete guidance for mankind. Quran is the last but not the only book that was ever revealed to mankind. Yet, in our times, while no other Divine Book is available in its original pure form, Quran is the only Divine Book that has remained intact in exactly the same form and text as it was originally revealed.

Through the ages, within scholarly circles of all faiths and creeds, the assertion that this Glorious Revelation is the most reliable, valid and authentic manuscript has always remained an irrefutable fact. Each and every word, even the individual alphabets and their punctuation signs have been preserved without the slightest alteration, admixture or adulteration whatsoever. Moreover, it has been preserved not only as a written document, but also in the memory of countless Muslims at all times, from generation to generation and from place to place for the last fourteen centuries. In fact, the Quran is the only book that has been preserved and transmitted through the memory of countless persons. This has further ensured the authenticity of the Quran.

Authenticity and truth of a finding or report is usually judged by two scientific criteria. These criteria are:

1. "Reliability" (reproducibility) and
2. "Validity" (accuracy).

Webster's dictionary (1997) defines "reliable" as "trustworthy" and "valid" as "sound and logical". Similarly, Oxford dictionary (1995) defines the word "reliable" as "able to be relied upon", and the word "valid" as "having legal force, sound to the point and logical".

We can clarify these concepts of reliability and validity by using a common example. Suppose a radio advertisement states that every item in a certain store is on sale for fifty percent off. Several people who hear this ad pass this information on to others, who in turn pass it on to some other persons. Now if the information that is passed from one person to the next is identical then it will be considered "reliable". Furthermore, if customers, who go to the store, find that everything is indeed on sale for fifty percent off, then this information will be considered "valid" as well. From this example it is easy to conclude that even though reliability and validity are related terms these terms are not mutually interchangeable. Thus, while transmission of some information may be considered "reliable" it is not necessary that the same information should be "valid" as well, and vice versa.

In the light of the above analogy, let us first examine the "reliability" of the Quran. If evidence proves that no change has occurred in the transmission of the Quran from generation to generation and from place to place and that the form and text of the Quran today is exactly the same as it was when it was revealed to the Prophet Muhammad (PBUH) then, from our perspective, this will establish the "reliability" of the Quran. In the following pages, reader will find abundant historical evidences that should more than suffice to establish the "reliability" of the Quran in absolute terms and beyond any shadow of doubt.

RELIABILITY OF TRANSMISSION OF THE QURAN

From the very beginning of the revelation, two concomitant parallel channels were established for preservation and transmission of the Quran. First channel consisted of verbal memorization and transmission. The second channel was in the form of written documentation. Preservation of the Quran, therefore, is not dependent entirely upon paper record only. Memorization of Quran assures that even in the absence of any hard copy, each and every alphabet, word, sentence, punctuation, pronunciation and sequence of the Quran is eternally carved in the memory of countless believers. This is a continuous phenomenon by which Quran is transmitted orally, throughout out the world from generation to generation and from place to place. Through the millennia, this memorized record has served as a definitive and secure repository of the Quran. As a matter of fact, this is the ultimate gold standard against which all hard copies of the Quran are judged and credentialed for accuracy and authenticity.

ORAL TRANSMISSION BY MEMORIZATION

Prophet Muhammad (PUBH) was the first "Hafiz" (keeper, memorizer) of the entire Quran. He memorized every verse as soon as it was revealed. Sometimes, during early periods of revelation, he would try to repeat the verses hurriedly lest he may forget any of the revelation. So, to reduce his anxiety, Allah, the Exalted, sent him the following assurance:

> *Move not your tongue concerning (the Quran) to make haste therewith. Indeed it is upon Us (Allah) to collect it, and give you the ability to recite it (from your memory). So when We (Allah) have recited it, then follow its recitation. Then it is upon Us (Allah) to make it clear to you.* Qiyamah 75: 16-19

These verses clearly state that whatever was revealed to the Prophet (PBUH) was also preserved in his memory by the blessing of Allah. This enabled him to deliver the Quran to mankind in exactly the same form and text in which he received it from Allah.

Books of Ahadith (narrations from the Prophet PBUH) provide authentic reports that every year, during Ramdhan (month of fasting), Prophet Muhammad (PBUH) used to recite all of the

Quran that was revealed up to that time to angel Gabriel, who would then recite the same back to him. It is also reported that Prophet (PBUH) recited entire Quran from memory two times, during Ramadan, in the last year of his life. He also listened to the entire Quran two times from angel Gabriel in the same month. Books of history and Ahadith also state that Zaid bin Thabit, the chief scribe of the Quran, was present during the last recitation and listening of the Quran by Prophet Muhammad (PBUH). This process of annual review provided ultimate assurance and guarantee that accurate wording of the Quran remained in the memory of the blessed Prophet (PBUH) until the last day of his life.

Recitation of at least some verses of the Quran is an integral part of the five obligatory daily prayers. Hence, to perform their daily prayers, all of the Prophet's companions memorized at least some portion of Quran. Beyond the minimal obligations, memorization of Quran was an ongoing obsession of many companions of Prophet (PBUH) and numerous companions had memorized the entire Quran, during the life of Prophet (PBUH). Names of many of these illustrious souls have been accurately preserved in the pages of history books. This ensured the preservation of the Quran in the memory of the first generation of Muslims.

While leading three of the five daily prayers, Prophet (PBUH) used to recite a portion of Quran audibly, so that the followers could listen to his recitation. This enabled a large number of his companions to daily verify, directly from Prophet (PBUH), accuracy of portions of the Quran, that they had personally memorized.

Prophet (PBUH) also enjoined Muslims to learn and memorize the Quran. There are numerous Ahadith that detail virtues of learning and teaching the Quran. For example, Uhtman bin Affan, a famous companion and third Caliph of Prophet (PBUH), reports that the Blessed Prophet (PBUH) said:

The most superior among you are those who learn the Quran and teach it to others ". (Bukhari)

As a result of these extolments, millions of individuals, since the time of Prophet (PBUH), have dedicated their entire lives towards accurate memorization and teaching of Quran. This has been a continuous process during the past fourteen centuries and there has never been a gap in this effort. Every Muslim generation for the last fourteen centuries had several Huffaz (plural of Hafiz) in every community. These persons orally transmitted the Quran to the next generation.

Taraweeh Salat is a special set of prayers offered every year during the month of Ramadhan (fasting). It is a universal Muslim practice, which has continued since the time of Prophet's Companions. Usually a Hafiz (One who has memorized the whole Quran) leads Taraweeh Salat in congregation. During these special prayers, he recites the whole Quran from his memory. It is a common practice of this prayer that a number of other Huffaz stand in congregation behind the leading Hafiz. These Huffaz intently listen to the recitation of the leading Hafiz and provide spontaneous correction for any mispronunciation, mistakes, sequential misplacement or omissions of the verses of the Quran during his recitation.

In the presence of such over whelming system of checks and balances it is absolutely inconceivable that any deviation from the original could ever have interjected in the text of the Quran, or if such an attempt is ever made, that it can survive scrutiny from hundreds of thousands of Huffaz present in every Muslims community.

WRITTEN TRANMISSION BY DOCUMENTATION

It is a well-documented fact that as soon as Prophet Muhammad (PBUH) received a revelation of the Quran, he used to dictate it to one of his scribes. This created an immediate written record of the revelations. In addition to recording the revelation, Prophet

(PBUH) would also instruct the scribe, the exact place of the revealed verses in the text of the Quran i.e. inclusion of verses within a specific chapter and order of verses in that chapter, e.g. he would instruct the scribe to write down the revealed verses in chapter 10 following verse 27 of the chapter. After dictation, the scribe was asked to read the verses back to the Prophet (PBUH) to confirm that all verses have been documented accurately. Historians have preserved names of more than 40 persons who served as scribes of the Quran. Among this group, Zaid bin Thabit has been distinguished as the chief scribe.

An incident which took place during the early years of revelation in Makkah provides proof that the Quran was preserved in written from the very beginning of the revelation. The incident relates to Umar ibn al Khattab, the second Caliph, who at that time was an avowed enemy of Islam. One day he set out intending to find and kill the Prophet (PBUH). On the way someone told Umar that his sister and bother in-law had already accepted Islam. So, before attempting to kill the Prophet (PBUH), first he ought to set his own house in order. Upon hearing this, Umar rushed back to his sister's home. When he reached his sister's house he heard voices of recitation. Suspecting that his sister and her husband were reading the Quran, he attacked both of them in a violent manner. His sister was injured and started bleeding. Even so, she challenged Umar that, even if he was to kill them, she and her husband would never give up Islam. The sight of his battered sister and her determination touched Umar's feelings. He demanded to see the inscriptions that the couple was reading but his sister refused to let him touch the Quran unless Umar purified himself physically. Umar complied, and then read the document, which consisted of a few verses of chapter 20 of the Quran. He was so struck with the truth of the message that he went straight to Prophet (PBUH) and embraced Islam. This incident shows that the Quran was documented in writing even during the earliest period of revelation.

A number of Ahadith prove that, during the time of Prophet (PBUH), written copies of the Quran were readily available in Medina. According to one of these Ahadith, when a visitor came to Medina, he was given a copy of the Quran so that he could learn about Islam by himself. Also, according to another narration the blessed Prophet (PBUH) has said:

> *Do not take the Quran on a journey with you, lest it falls into hands of an enemy (who might desecrate it).* (Muslim)

Details of the last pilgrimage of the Prophet (PBUH) are preserved in several books of Ahadith and history. During this pilgrimage the Prophet (PBUH) delivered his famous "Farewell Address" to a gathering of about 124,000 Muslims. In his farewell address the Blessed Prophet (PBUH) said:

> *I am leaving behind with you two things; if you hold fast to them, you will never go astray; the book of Allah and the practice of His Prophet.* (Muslim)

It is clear that the Prophet (PBUH) would not have used the word "Book of Allah" unless, at that time, the Quran was not already available as a written document.

Quran itself testifies that it exists in the form of a written book.

> *(This is a) Book that We (Allah) have sent down to you, full of blessings, so that they (men) may ponder over its verses, and that men of understanding may be reminded.* Mujadila 38: 20

That the Quran is a book is also stated right at the very beginning of the Quran itself

> *Alif.Lam.Meem. This is a Book in which there is no doubt.* Baqara 2: 1-2.

In the text of Quran, Arabic word Kitab (book) is used more than 80 times, to describe the Quran.

Based on the above information it is logical to conclude that the entire Quran was preserved in the form of written documents during the lifetime of Prophet Mohammad (PBUH).

Role of the first Caliph Abu Bakr: 10- 13 AH (632-635 AD)

Abu Bakr became the first caliph (successor) after Prophet Muhammad (PBUH) passed away in 10 AH (632 CE). During the first year of his caliphate, in 11 AH, seventy *Huffaz* (those who memorized the entire Quran) were martyred in the battle of Yamamah. This was an alarming loss of Huffaz in the first generation of Muslims. As a result of this incident Umar ibn Al-Khattab came to the conclusion that memorization alone was not enough to safe guard the preservation of the Quran. He asserted that complete text of the Quran must also be secured as a written document in a single volume so that it can serve as an unambiguous reference for future generations. Umar approached Abu Bakr and persuaded him to undertake such a compilation.

Abu Bakr initially refused to consider any undertaking that the Prophet (PBUH) had not done during his life. One apparent reason for not compiling the entire Quran in a single book format during the life of Prophet (PBUH) was that, while the Prophet (PBUH) was alive, the Quran was being revealed continuously. The Prophet (PBUH) did not have an ability to predict when next verses of the Quran would be revealed and where these verses would be placed in the text of the Quran. Revelation of the entire Quran was completed before the Prophet (PBUH) passed away. Hence it became possible to collect all parts of the Quran and rewrite them together in the form of a single book.

Abu Bakr later understood this need and concurred with the proposal of Umar. He then instructed Zaid bin Thabit, the chief scribe of the Prophet (PBUH), to collect individual written documents of the Quran, rewrite them, and assemble them together in the form of a single book.

Zaid accepted the assignment and adopted the following method to carry out his mission diligently: He made a general announcement that all those who possessed any portions of the Quran in the written form should bring these documents to him. Zaid was a Hafiz of the Quran but to avoid taking any chances he did not rely on his own memory alone. Therefore, whenever any written portion of the Quran was presented to him, he would compare it with other records of the same written portion. Then to rule out any contradicting evidence he would make public announcement that he has received a specific portion of the written Quran e.g., he would announce that he has received a written portion of Chapter 9, verses 10-15. After this, to remove even the remotest possibility of error, he would perform another cross check with an alternate standard. He would invite more than one person, to recite the same verses from memory. The general rule for the acceptance of any written document was that a written document would be considered authentic only if at least two reliable persons could recite the same passage from memory in the exact same form. By these means Zaid was able to assure reliability and authenticity of each and every word of the Quran. After completion of collection and verification of individual written documents of the Quran, Zaid rewrote and assembled all verses of the Quran in the form of a single book.

This copy of the Quran was then entrusted to Hafsa, one of the wives of the Prophet (PBUH), for safekeeping. From that time onwards this copy of the Quran became the official reference book against which all Quranic writings that existed at that time could be compared and authenticated.

Role of the third Caliph Uthman: 24-35 AH (644-655 CE)

By the time of the third Caliph Uthman, Islam had spread far and wide. Muslims who belonged to distant and different places began to read the Quran in their specific local dialects. Serious differences then arose among Muslims of different places about the proper recitation of the Quran. Uthman then realized the need for bringing uniformity in the recitation of the Quran. He entrusted Zaid bin Thabit along with three other scribes of the Prophet (PBUH) to rewrite the Quran in the dialect of Quraish, the tribe in which Prophet Muhammad (PBUH) was born. Zaid acquired the original copy of the Quran from Hafsa. Based on this Quran, he scribed seven copies of the Quran in Quraish dialect. Later, Uthman sent one copy of this Quran to each of the six different regional centers of the Muslim state and kept one copy in Medina. Along with each copy of the Quran, he also sent a professional "Qari" (reciter) who could recite the Quran in Quraish dialect. This brought about a complete uniformity in reading and scribing of the Quran for the entire Muslim world. Two copies of the Quran written at that time are still available. One is at Tashkent in Central Asia and the other at Istanbul in Turkey. The fact that no change at all has occurred in the text of the Quran during the last fourteen centuries can be ascertained by comparing the present day copies of the Quran throughout the world with these original copies of the Quran.

Ibn Hazam, the famous Muslim scholar, stated that at least 100,000 copies or portions of the Quran were documented during the period of Uthman (1). The history also shows that many copies or portions of written Quran were freely available in the Muslim world. A famous battle called "Siffin" took place in the year 36 AH (657 CE) during the Caliphate of Ali. This was a non-conclusive battle that went on for several days. One party of the battle then put portions of the Quran on their spears. This spectacle quickly brought the battle to an end. This incident is reported by Muslim as well as non-Muslim historians, and provides further evidence that many copies or portions of the written Quran were freely available to Muslims even on battle fields.

---

1) The Quran & Gospels by Dr. Laylah, published by El-Falah Foundation, Houston, 1998.

Role of Tab'ien:
Generation following Prophet's Companions

The Arabic script used in the seventh century, i.e. during the period of the Prophet (PBUH) and his companions consisted of very basic symbols, which expressed the consonantal structure of the alphabets but did not facilitate clear reading and pronunciation of the specific words. Several Arabic alphabets were written by a single mark or line, such as ba, ta, tha and ya. Only an experienced person could read this script. Two important measures were introduced by "Tab'ien, which further ensured the uniform recitation of the Quran. Technically, these are known as "Tashkeel" and "Nuqat". "Tashkeel" refers to the diacritical signs indicating the vowels. In Arabic they are known as fatha, kasra and dhamma and in Urdu as zabar, zaer and paish. Tab'ien added these signs to each and every alphabet in the text of the Quran prepared by Uthman. This was a monumental task, which enabled even a non-Arabs to correctly read each word of the Quran, e.g. when alphabet b is joined with a, this could be distinctly read as ba, bee, or bu depending on the diacritical signs or "Tashkeel" put on b.

"Nuqat" refers to the placing of appropriate dots with each alphabet, e.g. ba was given one dot, and ya given two dots at the bottom. Similarly ta and tha were given two and three dots respectively at the top. This remarkable work was done during 66-86 AH (685-705 CE). The addition of "Tashkeel" and "Nuqat" ensured an absolute uniformity in the documentation and recitation of the Quran even by those whose mother tongue is not Arabic.

It is evident from these illustrations that the Quran was faithfully preserved and transmitted by its believers by two different and independent means; oral and written. Whereas no change was needed in the oral transmission of the Quran, several improvements were made in the written transmission of the Quran. These improvements not only preserved its text but also brought an absolute and universal uniformity to the recitation of the Quran. The fact that no change has occurred in this transmission during the last fourteen centuries can be ascertained by looking at the two original written copies of the Quran still present in the world. At the same time this could also be ascertained by listening to the recitations of the Quran by several Huffaz from different parts of the world. The Quran thus meets the criterion of reliability through two independent means i.e. its transmission through memorization and through documentation. In fact, the Quran is the only Divine Book that meets the factor of reliability without the least shade of doubt.

It should, however, be noted that the criteria of reliability or validity are human measures. Hence we should not in any way judge a Divine Book by human standards. As very truly stated in the foreword, the Quran is a Divine Book, and should be accepted as such. Therefore, it is essential to emphasize that the above illustrations are a means only to educate a common reader and not to evaluate the reliability or validity of the Quran. The fact is that Quran is the absolute truth from the Creator of the worlds and does not need human scales to prove its reliability as a Divine Revelation from Allah, the Exalted.

Chapter Two

VALIDITY OF THE QURAN

A Divine act stands as an absolute truth on its own merits. Truth of a Divine act is not dependent upon any human acknowledgement or verification. The Quran is a Divine Book and a living miracle of Allah, the Exalted. Acknowledgement or denial of this fact by an individual or the entire human race can neither add to nor subtract any thing from this Divine Truth. Moreover, mankind has no mental capability, scientific tool or research technique, which can prove that a Divine act can be accomplished or evaluated by any non-Divine entity. In realty all arguments which purport to claim otherwise can be proven to be nothing more than misguided conjuncture or an exercise in circular logic. As such, the following discussion should not be misconstrued as an attempt to prove or disprove Divine origin of the Quran, rather it should be comprehended as a discourse for gaining some understanding of the validity of the Quran as a Divine Revelation.

The word "miracle" in dictionaries is defined as a Divine Act. Allah, the Exalted, alone has the power and wisdom to initiate and manifest any miracles. Thus, in a nascent, pristine sense, no human being can ever initiate or perform any miracle by his/her own will, power or capability. Now, if we can establish that the language and the information in the Quran could have not come from any human source, then, for our purposes, this fact would constitute a proof that the Quran is a miracle. This would then satisfy our quest for validating our knowledge of Quran as a Divine Revelation from Allah, the Exalted.

Most of the verses in the Quran are very clear and explicit. On the other hand, a few verses describe concepts or use terms that are not fully understood by a certain generation of mankind. The Quran describes them as allegorical verses. Needless to mention, the level of knowledge of every human generation corresponds with its understanding of science and technology. Hence every human generation finds a few allegorical verses in the Quran. Allah, the Exalted states in the Quran.

It is He who has sent down the Book; in it are verses basic and fundamental; they are the foundation of the Book; others are allegorical. Al-e-Imran 3: 7

Each Muslim generation accepted the allegorical verses as Divine expression of mysteries of universe. As human knowledge advanced to higher levels of understanding, each successive Muslim generation has been able to decode the concepts hidden in a few allegorical verses, thereby changing the mysteries of the Quran to facts of science. Each Muslim generation decoded a few allegorical verses of the Quran that corroborated with its level of knowledge in science, and technology. The same verses for the previous generations were mysteries, but became facts for their own generation. This has been a perpetual miracle of the Quran for the last fourteen centuries.

Human society comprises of a multitude of sectors. Moreover, members of human race have varied interests and diverse specialties. Quran is a book of guidance for the entire mankind. It therefore provides specific miracles and challenges for all sectors of human society and also addresses the varied interests of human race. The Quran provides miracles for those interested mainly in the language and diction. It also provides specific miracles for those interested in various domains of science such as chemistry, biology, astronomy, embryology, astrophysics etc. At the same time, it provides miracles for those interested in past history, future prophecies, and the countless mysteries of nature. In fact, this has been the most outstanding and unique miracle of the Quran.

The simple fact that Quran does not spare a single aspect of the basic needs of human race, and provides concise information, guidance and inspiration for each and every aspect of human life, is a manifest miracle by itself. In addition, this Glorious Book also contains precise facts about the mysteries of nature, various branches of science, past and future events of human history, and even those items which are not yet encompassed by the farthest reaches of human perception or fantasy. Lastly, the masterful, intertwined, organization of all of this universally encompassing information in a volume the size of Quran is, in itself, an awe inspiring miracle of boundless proportions. The fact that further adds to the miraculous nature of this Divine Revelation is the testimony that none of the discoveries of science, technology or history during the last fourteen centuries could find a single contradiction in the statement of the Quran.

On the following pages I have listed examples of some recently discovered facts in science, technology and history that corroborate with the information in the Quran. For further details reader can refer to two books that I have published earlier (1). Hopefully these glimpses of the yet unfathomed miracles of the Quran, will help the reader to appreciate the mysteries and miracles of the Quran. If a reader is able to discern the truth in any of these miracles, this should then establish the validity of the Quran as the Divine Revelation from Allah.

As stated earlier, whether a reader accepts or does not accept any of these mysteries and miracles, the Quran is the Divine Revelation from Allah. It is the absolute truth that does not need a human scale to establish its validity as a Divine Revelation.

MIRACLES IN THE LANGUAGE OF THE QURAN

1. Muslim and non-Muslim scholars readily acknowledge the fact that Prophet Muhammad (PBUH) never had any formal

---

1) Kazi, Mazhar. 130 Evident Miracles in the Quran
   Crescent Publishing House. Lefferts. New York. 1998
2) Kazi, Mazhar. 160 Miracles & Mysteries of the Quran
   Al Minar Books. Philadelphia, Houston. 2003

education, before or after the revelation of Quran. He (PBUH) had no occasion to spend any extended period of time in company of scholars, whether in Makkah or abroad. It is well known that, lacking didactic education, Prophet (PBUH) could not read, write or even sign his name. Yet, the Quran, in its entirety, is a unique monument of linguistic perfection, which has never been matched by any one at any time. This fact stands out even more strikingly when we realize that the Quran has repeatedly challenged the entire mankind, to produce even a single passage, which can match any passage in the Quran. Here it is noteworthy that the shortest passage in the Quran consists of only three verses. Yet, history bears witness that, even the best, most renowned, eloquent and prolific writers of the time were dumbfounded by this challenge. Each and every one of these super poets and linguistic experts was humbled into submission that indeed no human soul can ever produce any writing that can parallel or even come close to linguistic precision and qualities of the Quran. Incidentally, after one thousand four hundred years, this challenge is still open and remains unmet by any one.

2. It is a common observation that after a certain period of time every human language undergoes a gradual change and assumes an entirely new shape or form. Moreover, often the same language is written and spoken in different dialects in different countries.

Against all odds, Quran is still read and understood in the entire world in the same language in which it was revealed more than 1,400 years ago. Not a single word, phrase or idiom of this Book has become obsolete or lost its original meaning. Also, the language of the Quran has always maintained one universal dialect irrespective of differences in time and space. The fact that a book with such perfect, timeless language and a universal dialect was revealed through an unlettered Prophet is another living miracle of the Quran.

MIRACLES IN THE CHALLENGES OF THE QURAN

3. Find a contradiction in the Quran

Do they (the unbelievers) not reflect upon the Quran; if it had been from (someone) other than Allah, they would surely have found therein much contradiction. Nisa 4:82

Readers Digest issue of Dec.1952 states: "Modern scholarship had uncovered nearly 6,000 errors in the New Testament alone".

4. Produce a similar Quran

Say if whole of mankind and Jinn gathered to produce the like of this Quran, they could not produce the like of it, even if they backed up each other with help and support. Bani Israel 17: 88

5. Make a chapter like the one in the Quran

Do they say: He (Muhammad) forged it? Say: Bring then a chapter like unto it, and call (to your aid) anyone besides Allah, if you speak the truth. Younes 10: 37-38

6. Produce ten verses like those in the Quran

Or they say: He (Muhammad, PBUH) forged it; Say: Bring you then (at least) ten verses like unto it, and call (to your aid) whomever you can besides Allah, if you speak the truth. Hud 11: 13

7. Produce a recital like that of the Quran

Do they say: He (Muhammad) fabricated (the Quran), nay, they have no faith, let them then produce a recital like unto it, if they speak the truth. Toor 52: 33-34

MIRACLES IN HUMAN HISTORY

8. Preservation of Pharaoh's body

We (Allah) will save your body, so that you may be a sign for succeeding generations; though there are many who give no heed to Our signs. Younes 10: 92

These verses refer to Pharaoh. It should be noted that the Bible also states that Pharaoh had drowned in the sea but it does not give any information as to what happened to his body subsequently. The Quran affirms that his body was to be saved. It is now on display in a museum in Cairo, Egypt.

9. City of Iram

Have you not seen how your Lord dealt with 'Aad of Iram (who were very tall) like lofty pillars, the like of which no nation was created in the lands of the world. Fajr 89:6-8

The National Geographic magazine, December 1978, gave a detailed account of recent discovery of this city. No other religious or history book provides any description of people of Iram and their city, except the Quran.

MIRACLES OF SCIENTIFIC FACTS IN THE QURAN

The Quran details countless scientific facts and principles which, until recent scientific discoveries, were unknown to mankind. Therefore, in the absence of any other source of knowledge, without invoking the concept of Divine Revelation, it is impossible to explain how this kind of accurate futuristic information could have been incorporated in the Quran. In view of the absence of didactic education of the Prophet (PBUH) and his non-exposure to the scholarly pursuits, we have to conclude that the Quran is indeed a Divine Revelation which Allah, the Exalted has conveyed to us through His Messenger (PBUH).

Miracles in Astronomy

10. Beginning of the universe as a gaseous mass

He (Allah) comprehended in His design the heaven when it was (only) a smoke. Fussilat 41: 11

11. Origin of the universe as one entity

Have they not, those who disbelieve, seen that the heavens and earth were joined together (as one piece), then We (Allah) parted them. Anbiya 21: 30

12. Floating movement of planets in orbits

(Allah is the) One who created the night and the day and the sun and the moon; all (celestial bodies), float along, each in its (own) orbit. Anbiya 21: 33

13. Expansion of the universe

With power did We (Allah) construct the heavens? We are (continuously) expanding it. Zariat 51: 47

Miracles in Biology

14. Origin of life in water

Do not the unbelievers see that...We (Allah) created from water every living thing; will they not then believe. Anbiya 21: 30

15. Existence of opposite genders in all plants

And it is He (Allah) who spread out the earth and set thereon mountains standing firm and (flowing) rivers and fruits of every kind He made in pairs, two and two. Ra'ad 13:3

We (Allah) sent down rain from the sky and produced on the earth every kind of noble species in pairs.
Luqman 31: 10

Miracles in Human Beings

16. Presence of sensory nerves in skin

Those who reject Our signs, We (Allah) shall soon cast them into fire, as often as their skins are roasted through, We shall change it for them with fresh skin that they may taste the penalty (of Fire), For Allah is Exalted in Power, Wise. Nisa 4: 56

17. Uniqueness of finger-tips (finger prints)

Does man think that We (Allah) cannot assemble his bones? Nay, We are able to put together in perfect order (even) the very tips of his fingers. Qiyama 75: 3-4

Miracles in Chemistry

18. Presence of opposite radicals and ions

Glory be to Allah, who created in pairs all things that the earth produces........... Yaseen 36:36

Miracles in Embryology

19. Origin of man by the sperm

Was he (man) not a mere sperm drop, which is emitted. Qiyamah 75: 37

20. Covering of embryo by three layers

   He (Allah) creates you in the wombs of your mothers in stages one after the other in three veils of darkness, such is Allah, your Lord and Cherisher. Zumur 39: 6

21. Development of embryo in stages

   He (Allah) makes you in the womb of your mother in stages one after another ……… Zumur 39: 6

   It is He (Allah) who created you in divine stages. Nahl 17: 1

MIRACLES IN MYSTERIES OF NATURE

22. Presence of ocean currents in sea water

   Who has made the earth firm to live in, made rivers in its midst, set therein mountains and made a separating barrier between two bodies of flowing water? Could there be a God besides Allah? Nay, most of them do not understand. Namal 27: 61

   He (Allah) has let loose the two oceans that they may meet together. Yet there stands between them a barrier which they do not transgress; So O assembly of Jinn and Men! Which manifestations of your Lord's Power will you deny? Rehman 55:19-21

One should note that Prophet Muhammad (PBUH) never experienced a sea voyage. All of his life he lived at Makkah and Medina. He did not even see an ocean in his entire life.

23. Decrease of land due to melting of polar ice

   See they not that We (Allah) gradually reduce the land from its outlying borders? When Allah commands

something, there is none to put back His command,...
Ra'ad 13: 14

Here it is appropriate to reemphasize that the Quran was revealed more than fourteen hundred years ago. At that time, human mind did not have any basis, which would have enabled it to imagine any of the hidden mysteries of science and nature that are revealed in the Quran. Also, it is an irrefutable fact that all determinations and conclusions based on human knowledge and experience change with the passage of time. Therefore, if Quran was a product of human scholarship or imagination then, at least, a few of its verses should have been proven wrong by this time. On the contrary we find that not a single factual discovery of science during the last fourteen centuries has ever contradicted a single verse of the Quran. In fact, each additional human discovery leads to further corroboration with the information already described in this treatise. The Quran is a Revelation from the Creator, therefore, it is reasonable to expect and conclude that only that information which is provided by the Creator can be the ultimate and universal truth. Thus we see, again and again, that every assumption which contradicts any statement of Quran is eventually proven wrong by further observation and analysis. The truth in the Quran, on the other hand, encompasses and over rides all barriers of time and space. This leaves us with no other options except to concede that Quran is indeed a Divine Revelation from Allah, the All Wise and the All Knowing, the Creator of every thing.

A FEW UNPARALLEL FEATURES OF THE QURAN

In addition to the miracles of the Quran mentioned above, this Divine Book has a few unique features, which are not shared by any other Divine Book that was revealed before.

1. Original texts of all earlier Divine Books are lost and only translated versions of these books exist today. The Quran is the only book that exists in its original language. It should

also be noted that no question has ever been raised about the reliability of the original Arabic text of the Quran.

2. All existing versions of the earlier Divine Books are corrupted by man. Several original words of God are missing from the text, while several words which are the product of human thought have been interjected in indeterminate proportions. Scholars of all other faith agree that their respective reference Divine Books have been corrupted by man made narrations, statements and declarations which are juxtaposed with God's Words in a manner which makes it difficult to distinguish one from the other. To illustrate this point here is a quote from an article published in the Tuesday, Dec 23, 1993 issue of the Herald Tribune International. "Away from Politics: An Oregon State University scholar, Marcus Borg, whose study of Jesus set off a furor among fundamental Christians, got an endowed chair worth $ 3 million, one of the richest in religious studies. Mr. Borg is the author of a book contending that 80% of the sayings attributed to Jesus in the Bible were added by later authors".

In comparison to the above, the Quran is distinguished by the fact that no one has ever been able to cast a shadow of doubt on its authenticity. It is universally acknowledged by Muslims and Non-Muslims that the text of the Quran has remained unchanged since its revelation and it has suffered no adulteration at any time.

3. The original manuscripts of all previous Divine Books have been lost and none of the current versions can be traced back directly to the Prophet who received it. Also, there is no valid historical record, which can prove an unbroken chain of documentation and transmission of these Books through successive generations.

On the other hand, evidence proving that the text of the Quran can be traced back directly to Prophet Muhammad

(PBUH) is so voluminous, strong and convincing that even the harshest critics of Islam have been unable to deny this fact.

4. Another outstanding feature of the Quran is that it was revealed to Prophet Muhammad (PBUH) over a period of 23 years. Historians and commentators of the Quran have painstakingly assembled, documented, authenticated and preserved details of time, place and events relating to revelation of each passage of the Quran. No such data is available for any other Divine Book.

5. All earlier Divine Books were revealed in languages that are now dead or obsolete. Hardly any nation or community speaks these languages today. Therefore, even if any of these books could be found in their original languages, it will not be possible for a common man to read and comprehend their texts. The Quran was revealed in the Arabic language. Arabic is still a living and vibrant language. Countless people, communities and nations speak and understand this language. It is also taught in schools, colleges and universities throughout the world. Hence people of all ages, races and nationalities can easily read and comprehend the text of the Divine Guidance in its original language.

6. All previously revealed Divine Books were sent as guidance for specific sectors of mankind and their commandments were meant for groups of people defined by tribe, geographical area or an era of time. The Quran on the other hand addresses the entire humanity, present or future, and its commandments transcend all barriers of creed, time and space. The Quran repeatedly addresses its readers as, "O Mankind !".

7. Words of Allah, the Exalted, are always pure and consist of highest principles of morality and ethics. Man has contaminated all former Divine Books, by introducing base thought and expressions in the text, to the extent that he has

added obscenity and even incest to the words of God. One can find such immoral stories and descriptions in all former Divine Books e.g. Bible states that Prophet Lot got drunk and had sex with two of his daughters (Genesis 19: 30-36). Allah, the Exalted, has kept the Quran free from contamination by any form of obscenity. Not a single verse of the Quran contains even a trace of immoral or obscene description.

8. One of the most unique features of the Quran is that it is the only Divine Book that can be and has been memorized by millions of men, women and children. It is noteworthy that such memorization includes not only every word of the Quran, but also the punctuation marks and diacritical signs associated with each and every syllable of the Quran. This fact stands out even more strikingly when we realize that Arabic is not a native language for 88% of the total Muslim population and yet, even those who do not understand Arabic language can and do memorize the Quran in its entirety. Furthermore, even blind persons, who can not see the written words with their diacritical signs, can memorize the Quran with all of these details. This fact defies all conventional logic and reasoning and cannot be explained without invoking the concept of Divine intervention and Miracle.

9. Opening chapter of the Quran is a short but comprehensive supplication wherein a servant asks Allah SWT for guidance to the path of Success. The entire Quran following this opening chapter is Allah's answer to this supplication. Thus the very first sentence following this supplication reads:

Alif. Lam. Meem. This is the Book, there is no doubt in it (about it), a guidance for the God conscious.
Baqara 2:1-2

Quran is the only existing Book in the whole world that begins with this unique claim; "*there is no doubt in it* (or about it)". In order to appreciate this claim we need to understand the concept of the word "doubt". There can be three types of doubts about a book:

i) Doubts about the origin of the book
ii) Doubts about the internal consistency of the book
iii) Doubts about the external consistency of the book

So for the origin of the Quran is concerned, no rational mind can attribute the language, subject matter, scientific discoveries, past history, and prophecies of the Quran to Prophet Muhammad (PBUH), as an unlettered person. Therefore, reason and logic demand that we accept the origin of the Quran as a Divine Book from Allah, the All-Knowing and the All Wise. In other words there should not be even a trace of doubt about the origin of this book as a Divine Revelation. The Quran puts forth this claim in a very challenging tone:

And this Quran is not such as could ever be produced by any one other than Allah, but it is a confirmation of which was (revealed) before it, a fuller explanation of the Book, where in there is no doubt, (as a revelation) from the Lord of the worlds. Younes 10: 37

Internal consistency of a book means that various statements in its text should not contain any contradictions in the subject matter. All other books of faith, including Bible contain many such contradictions. But, the Quran claims:

Do they (the unbelievers) not consider the Quran (with care)? Had it been from someone other than Allah, they would have surely found much discrepancy therein. Al-Nisa 4: 82

This is a universal challenge to all unbelievers, which has survived the test of time. No one has yet discovered a single discrepancy amongst the various verses in the Quran. Hence no doubts can be raised regarding internal consistency of the Quran.

External consistency of a book means that there should be no contradiction between the assertions in the book and factual knowledge gained from sources outside the book. As human knowledge has advanced to higher levels of understanding and technology, for the past fourteen centuries, no one could yet point to even a single discovery in science and technology that contradicts information contained in verses of the Quran. Hence there should not be any doubt in human mind about the external consistency of this Book.

The above discussed unique and unparallel features of the Quran lead us to a final conclusion that by all scales of human understanding, reason and logic the Quran is indeed a Divine Revelation of Allah, the All-Wise and All-Knowing. Therefore, in view of the evidence presented, the prudent course of action should be to honor and obey the Commandments of the Creator contained in this Divine Book.

Chapter Three

A GLIMPSE INTO THE MYSTERIES OF THE QURAN

Literary persons often show off their talents and command of language by composing prose and poetry in which choice of words and their sequences are contrived to refer to and convey certain special connotations. In English language, mnemonics are the simplest forms of such linguistic exercises. Other examples of this nature include palindromes, anagrams, and panagrams. Arabic, Persian and Urdu poets often produce poetic descriptions of events where sum of numerical equivalents of alphabets denote date of the event. However, all such examples consist of only single words, single sentences, or short pieces. These items have no relation to one another and do not share a common theme.

In recent years scholars of linguistic in the Quran have found numerous examples of surprising numerical correlations, which are beyond human literary capabilities, dexterity or command. These are not confined to a single word, verse or a short piece, but spread through out the entire text of the Quran. A few examples of such numerical correlations are listed below.

MIRACLES IN NUMERICAL SYMMETRY OF THE WORDS IN THE QURAN

1. The Quran states that there are seven heavens. This description appears only in seven chapters of the Quran.

2. The Quran states that the number of months prescribed by Allah is twelve. The Arabic word *Shahr* meaning month appears in the Quran a total of 12 times

3. Arabic word *Eman* means faith. It appears in the Quran 17 times. Arabic word *Kufr* means denial. This also appears in the Quran a 17 times in the Quran. One of the derivatives of *Eman* is *Emanun* and that of *Kufr* is *Kufurun*. Each of these words appears 8 times in the Quran.

4. Arabic word *Malaika* means angels. It appears in the Quran 88 times. Arabic word *Shaitan* refers to devil. This also appears in the Quran 88 times. .

5. Arabic word *Dunya* means world. It appears in the Quran 115 times. The word *Akhira* means the world hereafter. It also appears in the Quran 115 times.

6. Arabic word *Teen* means clay and *Nutfa* refers to sperm. The Quran states that man is created from *Teen* and *Nutfa*. Each of these terms is used a total of 112 times in the Quran.

7. *Rahman* and *Raheem* are two names of Allah. The former refers to Allah's mercy associated with justice, and the later refers to mercy associated with forgiveness. The word *Rahman* appears in the Quran a total of 57 times, but the word *Raheem* appears a total of 114 times, the exact multiple of 57. This relationship corresponds with Ahadith that state the mercy of Allah overcomes his wrath.

8. Arabic word *Rijal* means man. Arabic word for woman is *Nisa*. The total number of each of these words used in the entire text of the Quran is equal, i.e. 24.

9. The Arabic word for life is *Hayat* and for death is *Mat*. Both appear in the Quran in exact same numbers, i.e. 145.

10. The Arabic word *Zakat* refers to Islamic charity or poor-due and the word *Baraka* mean increase in blessings. Both words appear in the Quran in exact same numbers, i.e.32.

11. Here is a very surprising correlation of a geological fact that needs a little decoding. The word sea in the Quran appears 32 times and the word land appears 13 times. Adding these two figures gives a figure of 45 that represents the total area of sea and land. 32 out of a total of 45 equals 71.1% which represents the area of sea%, and 13 out of 45 equals 28.8% which represents the area of land. Modern science has recently proved that water covers 71.11% of the earth, while the land covers 28.89%

MYSTERY OF TWO DIFFERENT INTERJECTIONS IN THE QURAN

12. The use of word *Thumma* in the text of the Quran is another enigmatic mystery. The Arabic word *Thumma* means later. It refers to a change that takes place after a pause. Where ever the Quran gives a description of stages of embryonic development of a fetus, the word *Thumma* appears only three times. The embryologists have now discovered that human embryo grows develops in three distinct stages. Thus the three embryonic stages of development were referred in the Quran centuries before scientists were able to discover this fact by microscope.

13. The Quran states that human embryo goes through different stages of growth. While describing these stages the Quran alternately uses two different interjection, namely *fa,* and *thumma,* The word *fa* can be translated as "then" referring to a change that place immediately, and the word *thumma* can be translated as "later" referring to a change that place after a pause. As mentioned earlier, while describing these changes, the Quran always uses the interjection *thumma* only three times. In between two *thummas* the Quran uses another interjection *fa* in varying numbers. In other words the Quran acknowledges that there are three main stages of embryonic development that are distinct. This is shown by the word *thumma* denoting a stage that comes with a little pause. Each state in turn has sub-stages that are very short lived and

hence may vary in number. Hence the Quran uses the word *fa* varying number of times. The modern embryologists have discovered this fact after fourteen centuries.

At this juncture it is important to note that these numerical symmetries have been discovered only recently by using computer technology. This technology was unknown at the time of Prophet Muhammad (PBUH) and these correlations were unknown to the scholars before our time. The significant of this fact becomes all the more important when we realize that the Quran was revealed piecemeal over a period of 23 years. It is impossible for any human mind to simultaneously maintain, track, and account for relevant and meaningful numerical relationship for such a large number of varied subjects, over almost one quarter of century, so that the tally of all addressed subjects come up with a perfect score from every point of view and from all aspects of subject under discussion. Furthermore the mysteries of human embryo which the modern scientists have discovered by the use of an electron microscope corroborate with the text of the Quran add to the miraculous mysteries of the Quran. All of these findings again point to the fact that the Quran is the Divine Word of All-Knowing Master and Creator of the universe.

Chapter Four

AN OVERVIEW OF THE QURAN

Abridged and modified from, "Introduction to the Quran"
by A.A. Maudoodi (1)

Discussions on the following pages elaborate two issues that are related to study of the Quran. First part deals with specific features that are unique to the Quran. Unless the reader accepts these unique features of the Quran, he will not get the desired benefit just by reciting its verses. Second part endeavors to answer a few general questions that arise in the minds of novice students of the Quran.

A UNIQUE BOOK

All books authored by human beings deal with a certain domain of knowledge. The Quran, on the other hand, primarily deals with faith. It also deals with human knowledge but as references to reinforce the faith. Thus a book of faith has no valid comparison with any book of knowledge.

In order to follow subject matter of the Quran and to understand its text, the reader should realize that Quran does not present information, ideas or arguments about specific themes in a conventional style. Common arrangement of written books presents information divided into distinct chapters, each one then deals with the subject matter sequentially arranged in the form of introduction, discussion and conclusion.

The reader should open the Book with a clear understanding that the Quran does not follow this format.

1) A.A.Maudoodi. The Meaning of the Quran V.1.
   Islamic publications. Lahore. Pakistan. 1989

In contrast to the sequential method of human books, the Quran combines discussions of various, apparently unrelated, topics in a very impressive, eloquently blended style. Thus it gives moral instructions, lays down laws, invites mankind to monotheism, admonishes disbelievers and gives glad tidings to believers, all at the same time. Often we find same subject repeated in more than one ways and apparently unconnected themes follow one another. Often a new topic is introduced right in the middle of another theme in an amazing blend of ideas. Similarly, diction of the speaker and the addressee changes within the same discussions, producing an all encompassing flavor. There are no signs of division by sections, chapters, title or sub-headings any where in the whole text of the Quran.

A student of the Quran will notice that every discourse in the Quran has its own unique style. Historical events are presented but not as in a history book. Problems of philosophy and metaphysics are treated in a manner different from a textbook on the subject. Man and universe are mentioned in a language different from that of the texts of natural science. Likewise, the Quran follows its own method of solving cultural, political, social and economical problems. It deals with principles of law and constitution in a manner quite different from that of jurists or sociologists. Most of all, morality is taught in a way that has no parallel in human literature.

Unless one maintains a clear vision of the overall perspective and objectives that the Quran intends to achieve, a casual reader may fail to see coherence and relevance of ideas elaborated in separate discourses of the Quran. However, if reader accepts the fact that Quran is the only book of its kind; its literary style is not a copy of any other book; its theme and address is unique and that the Quran addresses the entire human race, past present and future, then gradually true benefits of the Guidance contained in this Divine Book begin to seep in reader's conscious mind and eventually, with the dawn of the absolute Truth, the person is left awe struck by the magnificence of the Message contained therein.

NATURE OF THE BOOK: A Divine Guidance

First and foremost, the reader should understand the basic nature of the book. Whether one believes it to be a Divine Book or not, one will have to consider, at the starting point, the claim that is put forth by the Book, and the person who delivered the Book, namely Muhammad (PBUH). Both claim that it is a Divine Book, a revelation from Allah, the Exalted. Whether a person accepts or rejects this claim, the reader first of all has to acknowledge the fact that mankind needs Divine Guidance to live a happy and peaceful life. Unless one acknowledges this fact, no Divine Book and especially the Quran can help the reader.

Allah, the Exalted created man with basic faculties of learning, speaking, understanding, and discerning right from wrong and good from evil. Allah, the Exalted granted man faculties to acquire knowledge that may help him live a peaceful and productive life. At the same time, He also gave man freedom of will, and choice as a test for his worldly life. Allah, the Exalted is most Merciful and Kind to His creation. So, when He endowed mankind with will and choice, He also provided them a code of Guidance in the form of Divine Books, so that good becomes distinct from the bad and truth from evil.

If man chooses to submit to the will of Allah, the Exalted, he will be successful in this world and in the hereafter. If he refuses to do so then he will be a failure in this world and in the hereafter.

Adam (peace be upon him), the first man sent to this world, was the first Messenger of Allah, who was given the first Divine Guidance. Following Adam numerous Messengers were sent in different parts of the world at different times. Each Messenger of

Allah proclaimed the same message to his people, i.e. believe in Oneness of Allah, the Exalted, and surrender to His Will. As human society went through a gradual process of evolution, there was a need for a revised and more comprehensive guidance. It was for this reason that countless Messengers were sent with Divine Guidance to different parts of the world and at different times.

Muhammad (PBUH) was the last Messenger sent by Allah, the Exalted, and the Guidance that Allah, the Exalted sent with him is the culmination and conclusion of all previous Books of Guidance to mankind. Thus the Quran stands as the final and eternal Guidance of Allah, the Most Gracious. The Quran states:

It was not (possible) for this Quran to be produced by someone other than Allah, for (it is) a confirmation of what was (revealed) before it, and it is a detailed description of the (former) Scriptures, about which there is no doubt, from the Lord of the Worlds. Younes 10: 37

CENTRAL THEME

With this understanding of the basic nature of this Divine Book, we now turn to the main subject, central theme, and objectives of the Quran. The subject of the Quran is man. It explains the principles that will lead him to success and warns him against those acts that will lead to eternal failure. The central theme is Divine Guidance that constantly invites mankind to follow the path of the Messengers. It repeatedly points out that all other paths invented by man are false and will lead to utter failure in this world and the world hereafter. The objective of the Quran is to invite man to a life style that will lead him to a happy and peaceful life in this world and that will earn him Allah's eternal blessings in the world hereafter.

As the objective of the Quran is to guide man and not to teach specifics of the narrow domains of any branch of knowledge, it does not concern itself with unnecessary details of nature, science, history or philosophy. Whether narrating the story of creation of heavens and earth, origin of mankind, mysteries of nature or facts of history, the Quran maintains its basic theme and objectives through out all discourses, narrations and advices. It invites man to Divine Guidance and skips all irrelevant details of nature, science, history, or philosophy. It returns directly to its central theme again and again utilizing all forms, styles, rhetoric and address, at the same time maintaining a balance between human logic, perception and faith. Thus with the understanding that Quran is the Divine Guidance of the Almighty Creator to His creation, the beautiful, concise, and magnificent style of the Quran becomes all too clearly understandable and abundantly enjoyable. Various apparently unrelated topics and verses of the Quran can be best compared to different pearls of the same necklace, where each pearl though different, adds to the beauty of the necklace. When the Quran is studied in this light, the whole of it is closely interconnected with its subject, theme, and objective. All of these run very smoothly throughout the entire text of the Quran.

BACKGROUND OF THE REVELATIONS

Prophet Muhammad (PBUH) completed his mission over a period of 23 years; first 13 years were spent in Makkah and last 10 in Medina. During this period the Quran was revealed gradually according to varying conditions of the mission of Prophet (PBUH) and needs of the emerging Muslim community. In order to gain in depth understanding and appreciation of all facets and aspects of specific topics, chapters, and verses of the Quran it is necessary that the reader should be well versed with the background of their revelation including social and historical conditions, and antecedents associated with each revelation. Historians and scholars have painstakingly sifted through legends on these issues and have preserved the entire history associated with the revelations. The science that deals with this aspect of the study of Quran is known as "Shan-e-Nuzool", meaning the reason for revelation. These details are not considered as part of the meaning or translation of the Quran, but are documented separately as a commentary or explanation of the Quran. Reader can find these details not in the text of the Quran, but in various commentaries of the Quran. The more a reader will be familiar with these details, the better will be his understanding and appreciation of the Quran.

Chapters Revealed in Makkah

In Makkah, the Prophet (PBUH) was surrounded by unbelievers and pagans. Thus early revelations primarily address those people who are idolaters or unbelievers. By and large Quranic revelations of Makkah period invite these people to three basic articles of Islamic faith, viz. unity of Allah, the Exalted, prophet hood of Muhammad (PBUH) and accountability of the Day of Judgment. These revelations challenge and refute the false beliefs and customs of paganism. At the same time they invite unbelievers to adopt and respect basic principles of morality, good conduct, and family ties. Simultaneously a portion of these revelations also strengthen the faith of the new converts who had recently accepted Islam.

Most of the early revelations are short, concise verses with a precise, incisive literary style, which is more logical than poetic. At the same time it is rhythmic and eloquent in a way that touches the heart and soul of the listener and reader alike. The universal truths in these verses are explained with a local flavor, drawing upon familiar examples from environment, traditions and history of the land and people. The tone and style of these verses is very objective, based on reason and logic. Prophet (PBUH) continued his mission in Makkah for 13 years, however, with the passage of time local opposition and animosity gradually became worse and sinister. Hence the tone of late revelations of that era changes from simple address to that of challenge and warning, declaring severe punishment for the unbelievers and promising boundless rewards for the believers.

Hence these verses also give detailed descriptions of the punishments in Hell and the blessings in Paradise.

As a result of the Prophet's mission, a few of the non-believers, and pagans were accepting Islam. Makkah thus had a small but continuously growing population of Muslims. They were firm in belief, but new in Faith. A good section of Makkan verses also address to these new Muslims, reinforce their Faith, and prepare them for further tests and challenges in life.

Chapters Revealed in Medina

The Makkah society mainly consisted of idolaters and pagans, mostly from the ruling class of Quraish tribe. In contrast the society in Medina was more complex. It was made up of three major entities. First, there was an organized Muslim community with an emerging Muslim state. Second, there were established tribes of Christians and Jews. The third components consisted of a sizable number of hypocrites. These were the unbelievers who professed to be Muslims but had no attachment to Islam. They had accepted Islam only because of its growing force. Pagans population did not constitute a significant entity in Medina. Hence most of the revelations during Medina period addressed issues relating to these three different sections of the society. These verses invite Christians and Jews to follow the truth in their own Scriptures, and to accept the Divine Message of Prophet Muhammad (PBUH). They warn hypocrite for their conspiracies against the Muslims and the Prophet (PBUH). Most of these verses, however, are addressed to the Muslims. They provide the necessary details of their personal conducts and social responsibilities, and their new role as the vicegerent of Allah, the Exalted.

A few of these verses give basic principles regarding their relations with Christians and Jews, allies and enemies. Similarly guidance is also provided for personal lives of believers; warning them against failure in their test as believers; and urging them to sacrifice their lives and properties for the cause of Allah. Other verses teach moral lessons in victory and defeat, adversity and prosperity, war and peace. Some revelations lay down laws dealing with personal, family and social life. A great deal of emphasis in these revelations is laid on the social obligations and duties of the Believers. As the revelations in Medina dealt with more extensive subject matter, most of these chapters are longer than those revealed at Makkah. In contrast to Makkah revelations, which carry a tone of sharp, matter of fact, decisive statements, warnings and challenge to the non-believers, the tone and style of the revelation of Medina period exudes with love and compassion since they are addressed to the Believers. The language of these verses is equally eloquent, but more poetic than the Makkan verses.

STYLE

Gradual revelation of the Quran started a new Muslim Ummah (nation) amongst a hostile background of unbelievers. This continued for 13 years in Makkah, leading to the establishment of an Islamic state in Medina, where this Glorious revelation continued for 10 more years. Portions of the Quran revealed at Makkah focused mainly on the basic articles of faith that relate to personal life, whereas those revealed at Medina focused on basic laws that govern the personal and social life. It is obvious that such a comprehensive and vibrant Book cannot have the format, style, language and the tone, which is followed by a worldly book. Its tone and style should not be monotonous, but should change according to the background of its revelations. Hence each and every section of the Quran has its specific style that reflects the changing condition of the Muslims Ummah.

It should also be noted that various portions of the Quran were not revealed as publications in the form of handouts or pamphlets. Rather, these were to be delivered like a sermon or lecture by the Prophet (PBUH). Each portion of lecture was related to a certain phase of Prophet's mission. The Prophet

(PBUH) was entrusted with a comprehensive mission. He had to appeal both to human emotions and intellect. He had to deal with people of different mental levels. He also had to address the varying needs of the Islamic movement. He had to inculcate his message into the minds and souls of his followers. He had to educate and train them, imbue them with faith and courage and prepare them to face the opposing forces. He had to prepare them to struggle, live and die for the love of Allah. As a result, he had to change their whole life --- their mind, heart, attitude, priorities, and their daily conduct. The Quran was revealed to help the Prophet (PBUH) achieve these objectives. Therefore the style and language of the Quran also matches the various objectives of the mission of Prophet Mohammad (PBUH), both at Makkah and at Medina.

This in turn also explains the reason why the same theme in Quran is often repeated over and again. A specific objective of the Prophet's mission demands that only those things be mentioned which are relevant to the need of the mission. As long as there is a need to achieve a goal, or the Muslim Ummah stays at a certain stage of its growth, the Quran keeps repeating the same message over and again. It is, however, the miraculous beauty of the Quran that these repetitions do not create the monotony of style or language. Each and every repetition at its own place is equally impressive, elegant and unique.

Also, since the Quran is the guidance for all humanity for all ages to come, the same message is presented with varying emphasis on different aspects of human intellect so that each and every mind with its varying capabilities can comprehend the message clearly. In addition, all chapters of the Quran contain references to its basic theme; unity of Allah, Mission of the Prophet (PBUH), and accountability of the Day of Judgment. At the same time, all of them inspire piety, fortitude, endurance, forgiveness, love and compassion. These basic human virtues could not be neglected at any stage of the Muslim Ummah. This further accounts for the repeated description of the same text in the Quran. Hence the reader should not compare the style and format of the Quran with the monotonous and sequential style of the worldly book.

ORDER

The Quran is not arranged and documented in the sequence of its revelation. Some unbelievers question the order in which the passages of the Quran are arranged. They are of the opinion that, after the Prophet's demise, his companions arranged the text of the Quran, merely putting the longer chapters first and the shorter ones towards the end of the Quran. Allah, the Exalted alone knows the wisdom of the arrangement of His Book. Nevertheless, a little pondering over the differences between the Makkan and Medni chapters may help us to appreciate some of the wisdom of the arrangement and order of the Quran.

Although the Quran was to be the guidance for all times, it had to be revealed piecemeal according to two factors: first, varying needs of the mission of the Prophet (PBUH); second, the growing needs of the Muslim society. It is obvious that the sequence of revelations of the Quran which reflected the above two factors could, in no way, be the same for its documentation after the completion of its revelation. Another order, suited to changed conditions of the Muslim Ummah, was needed. In the early stages of revelation, the Quran addressed people who were totally ignorant of Islam. Hence it had to teach them the basic articles of faith. The later revelations were primarily addressed to the Believers. These verses were focused on their basic duties, personal and social obligations and the laws to be implemented in the Muslim Ummah. Obviously the order of the complete Book had to be different from its chronological order. The new order is meant for the eternal needs of Muslim Ummah and mankind at large. First and foremost, the Quran has to address its Believers. It has to prepare them to carry its message to others. It also has to warn them of the evils that appeared among the followers of previous books and former prophets, especially the

Christians and Jews. It is for this reason that the longer chapters of the Quran, e.g. Baqara and similar Medni chapters, which deal with these topics, are placed in the beginning of the Quran.

In this connection, another factor should also be considered. It does not suit the purpose of the Quran that all chapters dealing with similar topics should be grouped together. The Quran deals with human life as a whole. One cannot divide it into discrete compartments. All factors of life are always interconnected. The order and arrangement of the Quran also reflect this basic human need. It is for this reason that Makkan verses are mixed with Medni verses and vice-versa; also the chapters revealed at the early stage of Muslim Ummah are intermingled with those revealed in the later stages. In this way the entire picture of the Muslim Ummah remains in focus at the same time. This could be another reason for the present order and sequence of the Quran.

Last but not the least, we must remember that the order and arrangement of the Quran is Divine. Whenever a verse was revealed, the Prophet (PBUH) would call a scribe and instruct him to write it down. He would then describe the position of the revealed verse in the text of the Quran. He would be very specific, and instruct the scribe to write the revealed verse after such and such verse in such and such chapter. It is a historical fact that the Prophet (PBUH) and his companions always recited and documented the Quran in the same order and sequence that we have today. Therefore, the assumption that the present order of the Quran reflects an arbitrary arrangement on the part of the companions of the Prophet (PBUH) does not hold any validity. The fact remains that the order of chapters in the Quran and the sequence of verses in each chapter were personally assured by Prophet Muhammad (PBUH) under the Guidance of Allah, the Exalted.

UNIVERSALITY

A casual reader may misconstrue that the Quran being in Arabic language is primarily addressed to Arabs, who lived at the time of its revelation. No doubt it often mentions those things which are related to Arab environment, culture and customs. However, nothing can be further than truth. Quran is guidance for the whole mankind. Its message is for all civilizations and it addresses the whole humanity. The examples and reference to things which appear to be related to Arabs also apply to all those who have lived in or are living in similar environments. Incidentally, groups of a sizeable population of human race with pagan mentality have always lived and continue to live in open natural milieu which is no different than that of the by gone Arab tribes.

A simple exercise will easily prove this point. I suggest the reader to take a pencil and underline those sections, which give an impression that the Quran is meant for Arabs only. He should then pick up those conditions, things and incidents that refer exclusively to Arabs. He will be amazed to see that their number as compared to the total text of the Quran is very small. He should also try to note down those moral principles, personal attributes, social obligations and legal codes that refer only to the Arabs. He will be amazed to find no such sections in the Quran. Most of all, he should note the approach that the Quran follows for its basic theme and objective. He will acknowledge that it does not mention the least about Arab culture, history, or customs. He will notice that the Quran takes a global approach that addresses the mankind at large. In fact, the Quran is the only book wherein its verses repeatedly state; "O Mankind"!

In this regard another point is noteworthy. Every ideology, social system and religion must make references to specific cases and visible examples. None of them can teach in abstract terms and attract human attention. It is simply impossible to build a model of life merely on abstract forms. The only proper method is to start a movement in a specific territorial region and put its abstract ideas in action to create a living model. If successful, this model will catch attention of other nations and, if valid, the people will implement it in their own lands. It was for this simple reason that the first model Islamic state was established in the Arabian Peninsula. This model was so successful that today Islam is the religion of more than a billion people all over the globe. In fact, majority i.e. 88 percent of existing Muslim population today consists of non-Arabs.

What truly distinguishes a national system from an international, and a temporary system from a permanent one is evident from the teachings of the Quran. A national system aims to establish its own superiority at the expense of the life, property and welfare of others. It presents principles, theories and laws, which, by their very nature, are not meant to benefit other people. On the contrary, an international system grants equal rights to all human beings. It also presents an ideology that is universally applicable. Moreover, the principles and theories of a temporary system change with time and space, whereas no change occurs in the teachings of a permanent system. From all of these perspectives, the Quran is a universal Book free from all barriers of space and time.

All that has been presented above refers only to the domain of knowledge, reason and intellect of the reader. One should, however, remember that the Quran is basically a book of faith. Whereas, one can increase his knowledge by efforts and struggle, Faith is a gift of Allah, the Exalted. He blesses it only to those who seek it sincerely. The ultimate benefit from the Quran will come to a reader when he approaches it with purity of mind and sincerity of heart. Quran demands an approach with love, respect and devotion that is due to a Divine Revelation. The reader should sincerely pray that Allah, the Exalted opens his heart to receive His Guidance as it is only Allah, the Exalted who controls the hearts of His creation.

Chapter Five

WAYS TO THE BLESSINGS OF THE QURAN

Abridged and modified from "Way to the Quran"
by Khurram Murad (1)

As you come to the Quran, you come to a new world, a world of boundless treasures of knowledge, wisdom, imagination, inspiration and illumination. It is beyond human power to describe or even to comprehend the ultimate wisdom and blessings of the Quran. It is Allah's ultimate blessing to mankind and the fulfillment of His promise to Adam (peace be upon him) and his descendents. Allah, the Exalted, states:

There shall come to you Guidance from Me, and whoever follows My Guidance, no fear shall be on them, neither shall they grieve. Baqara 2:38

The Quran is a shield that will protect you from all forces of evils and temptations. It is the light that will lead you to success and salvation in this world and in the Hereafter. It is a constant sanctuary that provides peace and tranquility during the daily struggle of your life. Most of all, it is the only way that will bring you closer to your Creator. It tells you all that you should know about your Creator, His unique Attributes, His Exalted Power, and His Divine Wisdom. It also tells you how He rules this universe, how He relates Himself to you and how you should relate to Him. At the same time, it also tells you how you should relate to fellow men and every other thing in His kingdom. In fact, it is the most comprehensive source for all of your physical,

---

1) Khurram Murad. Way to the Quran.
   The Islamic Foundation. Leicester, UK. 1992

emotional, moral and spiritual needs. All of these blessings and bounties of the Quran are like a hidden treasure. The Quran opens the doors of its treasures only to those who approach it with a depth of devotion, sincerity of intention and purity of purpose that befits its majesty and glory. Each and every word in the Quran is a Revelation from Allah, the Exalted. Only those, who give due respect and reverence to its Divine Majesty are privileged to benefit from this treasure. Only those privileged can gather its treasures who are prepared to devote themselves completely to its guidance and try their utmost to follow and obey its commandments. It would be a tragic misfortune if any one comes to the Quran and then leaves empty handed, with soul untouched, heart unmoved, and life unchanged. The blessings of the Quran are limitless but the measure of your fill depends entirely upon your intention and effort. So, at the very outset, make yourself deeply aware of what the Quran means to you and what it demands of you. Make a solemn determination to recite it with the respect it deserves as the word of the All-Mighty Allah, a desire to obey its commandments and a will to change your life accordingly. The Quran will then open its boundless and endless treasures to you

BASIC PREREQUISITES

A. Attitude of the heart and mind

1. Faith and conviction
   Come to the Quran with a deep and firm faith that it is indeed the revealed Message of Allah, the Exalted. You should always remain conscious that each word that you are reading has been directly sent by Allah, the Exalted, as a personal message to you. This constant awareness is vital for the development of the attitude to benefit from the blessings and wisdom of the Quran. Ponder over the Majesty, Glory and Power of Allah, the Exalted. You will then feel an awe and devotion as you recite His Words.

2. Purpose of recitation

Recite the Quran with no other purpose other than to come closer to your Creator and to seek His guidance and His pleasure. Seek guidance from the Quran for each and every step of your life. Each word in the Quran is a Revelation from Allah, the Exalted. Hence it requires a special level of respect and devotion as symbol of Allah's Glory and Majesty. One, who holds the Quran in his hand, yet seeks his guidance and inspiration from another source is only running after mirages. His efforts will bring forth no blessings from the Quran.

3. Accepting the truth

Accept every piece of knowledge in the Quran without the slightest hesitation, skepticism or doubt. It is the absolute Truth from Allah, the Exalted, the All-Wise. You have the right to enquire, reflect and ponder upon the contents of the Quran; in fact the Quran enjoins the believer to do so, but remember that what you cannot comprehend is not necessarily unreasonable. The Quran contains the absolute and the ultimate knowledge that is Divine. Human mind can never comprehend its vastness, wisdom and mysteries. One has the right to deny and question the validity of the Quran as a Revelation from Allah, the Exalted, but once you have accepted its Divine nature, you have no basis whatsoever to doubt even a single word of it. There must be a total surrender to all that the Quran states. Your personal opinion, belief, notions, emotions, whims and caprices have no place or role in overriding any statement of the Quran.

4. Willingness to change

Have the willingness and determination to change and mold your attitude, behavior and conduct in accordance with the teachings of the Quran. Mere intellectual exercise will never bring you anywhere close to treasures of the Quran. As you go through the words of the Quran, put these words in practice in your daily life. The Quran will then infuse into your heart and soul.

5. Seeking refuge with Allah

As you embark upon reciting this Divine Book, be aware of your eternal avowed enemy, the Satan, who will make greater efforts to deprive you of the Blessings of the Quran. He will try to pollute your intention, create doubts in your mind and lapses in your remembrance that this is the Majestic, Glorious Word of Allah the Exalted. Satan will try to create barriers between your soul and the Words of Allah and tempt you away from its Commandments. It is for this reason that Allah states in the Quran:

When you recite the Quran, seek refuge with Allah from Satan the rejected. Nahl 16:98

Begin the recitation of the Quran by saying; "I seek refuge with Allah from Satan the rejected" and go back to this supplication, whenever a negative thought creeps into your mind during its recitation.

6. Allah's infinite Mercy

Realize that it is Allah's Mercy that can help you to receive the ultimate Blessings from the Quran. Your intention and efforts are only the means, but the rewards and blessings of the Quran will come to you only through Allah's Mercy. So approach the Quran with humility and reverence; with a sense of utter dependence upon Allah's Mercy. Put your full trust in His Mercy and seek His Blessings at each and every step of your recitation.

7. Constant praise and gratitude

Pulsate yourself constantly with intense praise and gratitude to Allah, the Exalted, for His Blessings that He has guided you to reading and study of the Quran. The more you thank Allah, the Exalted, the more He will bless you from His

Bounties. Open your heart and soul and pray as you have been taught in the Quran;

Our Lord let not our heart swerve (from Your Guidance), after you have guided us, and bestow upon us your grace; indeed you alone are the One who bestows (of all good). Al-e-Imran 3:8

B. Presence of the heart

While reciting the Quran, you should try your best to remain focused on the Quran. Remember and realize that the Quran was revealed to the "heart" of the Prophet (PBUH). Allah, the Exalted states:

Truly, this (Quran) is a Revelation from the Lord of the worlds; which the trustworthy (angel Gabriel) has brought down upon your heart that you may be (one) of the warners. Shua'ra 26: 192-94

The Quran will enter into your life only when you open your heart to it. Stay away from mere intellectual exercises and pour all of your inner emotions, aspirations, reverence, humility and devotion to the words of the Quran. Only then you will have the blessing to receive treasures of the Quran.

The following few rules may increase the devotion of your heart to the Quran.

1. Closeness to Allah

The Quran states:

Whatever portion you may be reciting from the Quran, and whatever deed you may be doing, we are witnessing thereof when you are engrossed therein. Nahl 16: 61

It also states:

He (Allah) is with you wherever you may be.
Hadeed 57: 4

Keep your heart and consciousness alive to this reality that you are in the presence of Allah, the Exalted, and that He is very close to you and that He is witnessing and watching you constantly.

2. Listening to the Quran from Allah, the Exalted
The Quran is a direct Revelation of Allah, the Exalted. So while reading the Quran, try to feel that you are in the presence of His Majesty. To start with, feel as if you are listening to the Quran from the blessed tongue of the Prophet (PBUH). Then feel as if it is coming to you from angel Gabriel and lastly as if it is coming to you directly from Allah, the Exalted. Let this be a constant and never ending effort during the entire phase of your recitation.

3. Direct addressee of the Quran
The Quran is the Word of Allah, the Exalted. So know and feel that through Quran Allah, the Exalted, is personally addressing you and you are listening to the words of the Quran from Allah Himself. Let all the intermediaries recede and disappear between you and Allah, the Exalted. Open your heart and soul. Let each and every word be a direct communication from Allah, the Exalted, to you. The very thought of this direct communication will keep your heart riveted on to what you are reciting.

4. Posture and position
Make your outward posture reflect your inner humility, devotion and submission to Allah, the Exalted. There should be a difference in your posture and position while reading a worldly book, or a newspaper and the Words of Allah, the Exalted. Find a special place to sit down, a place that is pure and clean and away from distractions. Make some kind of

mental and physical preparations that you are going to hold a Divine Book in your hand and that you are going to read Words of Allah, the Exalted. Your posture and position should have some reflection of this attitude.

5. Purification of self and surroundings
Purify yourself and your surroundings as much as possible. The Quran states:

That is indeed an honorable recitation; in a book well guarded; which none can touch but the purified. Waqia 56: 77-79

You should, therefore, try to have the utmost purity before you even touch the Quran. Your body, your dress and also the place where you recite the Quran should be clean. Make ablution before touching the Book of Allah. A group of scholars hold that one should not even touch the Quran without having an ablution. You should also try to have the purity and sincerity of your intentions. At the same time, the purity of soul is equally important. You should try to stay away from sins as much as possible. If you happen to commit a sin, then first ask Allah's forgiveness and then open the Quran. Also be careful that while reciting the Quran, you are not wearing something that is Haram (unlawful) and your stomach does not contain something that is Haram. The purer you are, the more your heart will open to receive the blessings of the Quran.

C. Understanding and Reflection

It is vital that you should try your best to understand what Allah, the Exalted, is saying to you through the Quran. At the same time, you should reflect and ponder over what you recite therein. Reading of the Quran, even without understanding, is an act of virtue in its own right. However, this does not fulfill the purpose for which the Quran has been sent to you. It has come to vitalize your whole life, mold your personality, and lead you to a better state of life. The Quran encourages the reader and exhorts us to think, reason and ponder over its verses. It states:

When they are reminded of the verses of their Lord, they fall not deaf and blind there at. Furqan 25: 73

It also states:

Then (why) do they not ponder over the Quran, or are there locks on their hearts? Mohammad 47: 24

The following guidelines may help you to achieve these objectives.

1. Understand and reflect over the Quran as if it was being revealed to you today. Remember that each word of the Quran is as living and relevant today as it was on the day it was first revealed. As such, you should try to relate and apply it to your daily life. Do not take any verse of the Quran as merely a story or the knowledge of the past.

2. At least once in your life, read the entire Quran from beginning to end. This will give you an overall idea of the Book. Concentrate on its major issues like its theme, style and message. If you are reading its translation or *tafseer* (commentary), it is recommended that you study more than one translation and *tafseer* simultaneously. Remember, every translation and commentary has some strong and some weak points. There is no such thing as the perfect translation of the Quran in any language.

3. Try to learn Arabic at least to the extent that enables you to understand the general meaning and message of the Quran. It may appear to be difficult at first, but every effort in this regard will bring countless blessings from Allah, the Exalted. Remember that Quran is the original word of Allah in Arabic language. No translation or commentary can be a substitute of it. At least get acquainted with the specific

Arabic terms of the Quran that can not be translated in any language

4. Ponder and reflect on the portion of the Quran which you read. This requires reciting the Quran slowly and even repeatedly. You may also read the same verses from different translations and commentaries simultaneously or at different times. It is stated that the Prophet (PBUH) and his companions would often spend the whole night just repeating the same verse. The Quran has an endless ocean of inspiration, wisdom and blessings. Each recitation of the Quran with the proper attitude of the heart and the mind will hopefully lead you to a higher level of inspiration and wisdom.

5. Depth of knowledge that you may acquire from different *tafseer* (commentaries) of the Quran varies from one author to the next. Find a commentary that suits the level of your knowledge, and your basic objective. In general each commentary of the Quran focuses on a certain basic theme, e.g. one may emphasize the language of the Quran, another may focus on the history of its revelation, yet another may focus on deriving Islamic laws *(Fiqh)* from the Quran, etc. Seek help from a knowledgeable person to recommend an appropriate commentary of Quran for you. This will further help you to appreciate the in depth meaning and the wisdom of each and every word of the Quran, according to your interest in the Quran and also according to your intellectual level.

D. Internal participation

As stated above, the Quran was initially sent down to the "heart" or the inner self of Prophet Muhammad (PBUH). You will, therefore, reap its full blessings when you are able to involve your inner self in your recitation. This may not be difficult if you are mindful that you are reading the exact words from your Creator, in His very presence.

The Quran states:

We (Allah) are nearer to him (man) than his jugular vein. Qaf 50: 16

The more you will feel close to Allah, the Exalted, the more you will have an internal participation of yourself with the Quran. The following guidelines may help you achieve this level of recitation.

1. Receiving the Quran into your heart
   Remind yourself of what the Quran states of those who receive it with their hearts and how the Prophet (PBUH) and his companions immersed their inner self in its recitation. The Quran states:

   When they hear what has been sent down to the Messenger, you see their eyes overflow with tears; because of the truth they have recognized; they cry out, Our Lord! We believe; so do write down us among the witnesses (of this truth). Maida 5: 83

   It also states:

   When His verses are recited unto them, they increase their faith. Anfal 8: 2

   You may or may not achieve this level of inner participation. Nevertheless, you should be aware of the level you desire to achieve.

2. Desire for a personal change
   You have already accepted the Quran as the Guidance from Allah, the Exalted. You should now try to make it relevant to your personal life. Consider that each message is a personal invitation for you to change your life, your acceptance of criterion of right and wrong, your scales of hopes and fear, and your only path to pursue in life. The closer you bring

your daily life to the words of the Quran, the more you will receive the blessings of the Quran.

3. Sincere response

Your heart should now be spiritually alive and respond to various notes and themes in the verses of the Quran. Let your heart flow with the theme of its specific verses. As the Quran describes the mercy of Allah, His wrath, His warnings, His glad tidings, etc, your heart should reflect similar state of emotions and inspirations. Each theme of the Quran should create a similar wavelength of emotions and inspirations in your heart and soul. This may be easy for you to achieve if you recite a specific theme several times, before moving on to another section of the Quran.

4. Sincere expression

Your tongue should express the various states of your heart. Recall how the Prophet (PBUH) and his companions used to recite the Quran. They would say "glory be to Allah" after reciting verses that describe Allah's Majesty and Power; They would say "thanks be to Allah", after reciting the verses that describe Allah's Bounties and Mercies. They would seek forgiveness and refuge with Allah, the Exalted, after reciting similar verses. Hence each theme of the Quran should not only create an internal state of heart but should also find an expression in your tongue. Even if one does not feel an internal change, one should express with tongue an appropriate response to the theme of the Quran.

E. Living by the Quran

The basic purpose of the Quran is to guide you to the path of Allah, the Exalted, and to bring your life into His submission. As you recite the Quran you should also try to live by what it enjoins upon you and what it forbids for you. You cannot expect to get even close to the blessings of the Quran if you do not follow what it enjoins and forbids. In fact, one who recites the Quran and does not try to act upon it, may be more likely to incur the displeasure of Allah, the Exalted. The Quran and Hadith both state that such a person is not a believer in the Quran. Also you should not take the Quran as a miraculous medicine that will change your life in one sitting or in one day. Applications of the Quran are a life long pursuit. The Quran will bring a gradual change in your life, if you are patient, have the desire to change your life, and then make the proper efforts to achieve this goal.

F. The life of the Prophet (peace and blessings be upon him)

The Quran was revealed to us through Prophet Muhammad (PBUH) and he is the one who explained it to us. Therefore, to fully absorb the Quran into your heart and soul, you must get as close to the Prophet (PBUH) as you can. If you want to see the Quran as a living model, study the daily conduct and behavior of the Prophet (PBUH). Ayesha (RA), the Prophet's noble wife, stated that the conduct of the Prophet (PBUH) was nothing but the Quran. Moreover, in order to move close to the Prophet (PBUH), you should study his Ahadith (sayings), his Sunnah (conduct), and his Seerah (life history).

These suggestions and guidelines will help the reader to receive blessings of the Quran. A reader may follow those that he prefers and also add a few according to his personal needs. Nevertheless, the blessings of the Quran will come only to the one who makes a sincere effort to receive them.

Chapter Six

DIVINE TESTIMONIES ABOUT THE QURAN

And if you are in doubt as to what We (Allah) have revealed (Quran) to our servant (Muhammad, PBUH), then produce a Sura (chapter) like therein, and call your witnesses (supporters and helpers) besides Allah, if you are truthful (in your doubts). But if you cannot, and of a Surety you cannot, then fear the Fire whose fuel is men and stones, prepared for the unbelievers.
Baqara 2: 23

This prophesy of the Quran; *"of a Surety you cannot "* has firmly stood the test of time. No one during the last fourteen centuries has ever been able to meet this challenge.

Do they (unbelievers) not ponder on the Quran? If it had been from someone other than Allah, they would surely have found therein much contradiction. Nisa 4: 82

Since the time of its revelation until now, despite all research and advancement in human knowledge, no one has been able to find even a single contradiction in the Quran.

This Quran is not such as can be produced by other than Allah; but it is a confirmation of what was (revealed) before, and a fuller explanation of the (previous) Books; wherein there is no doubt, (that it is revealed) from the Lord of the Worlds. Or do they (unbelievers) say: "He (Muhammad, PBUH) forged it?" Say: "then bring forth a Sura (chapter) like unto it, and call upon (for assistance) whoever you can besides Allah, if you are truthful. Younes 10: 37-38

Or do they (unbelievers) say: "He (Muhammad, PBUH) had forged it (this Quran)?" Nay! They believe not. Let them then produce (at least) a recital like unto it, if they are truthful. Toor 52: 33-34

(O Muhammad, PBUH!): Say "If the whole of mankind and Jinn were to assemble together in order to produce the like of this Quran, they could not produce the like thereof, even if they backed up each other with help and support". We have explained every (kind of) parable for mankind in this Book, yet most men refuse to do anything except disbelief. Bani Israel 17: 88-89

(O Muhammad, PBUH!) Neither did you read any book before it (Quran), nor did you write any book (whatsoever) with your right hand, in that case, indeed, the followers of falsehood would have had (a cause) for their doubts (in the Quran). Ankabut 49: 28

Verily, it is We (Allah) who sent down the Message (the Quran), and surely, We will guard it (from any corruption). Hijr 15: 9

The Quran is the only Divine Book that Allah promised to guard. It is because of this promise that the Quran is still free of all human corruptions. Even Non Muslims acknowledge and admit that no change has ever occurred in the text of the Quran

It is He (Allah), who has sent down to you the Book (The Quran); in it are verses that are clear; they are the foundation of the Book; others are allegorical; those in whose hearts is deviation, follow the part that is allegorical, seeking discord and searching for its hidden meaning, but no one knows its hidden meaning except

Allah; and those who are firmly founded in knowledge, say: " We believe in the Book, the whole of it is from our Lord"; and none will grasp the Message except men of understanding. Al-e-Imran 3: 7

Verily this Quran does guide to that (path) which is most right, and gives glad tidings to those who believe and work righteous deeds; that they shall have a magnificent reward. Bani Israel 17: 9

Verily, We (Allah) have revealed the book in truth for mankind; So whoever accepts the guidance, benefits his own soul, but he that strays away injures his own soul. Zumar 39: 41

This is indeed a noble Quran, preserved in a Book well guarded. None shall touch it but those who are clean. It is a revelation from the Lord of the Worlds. Is it such a Message that you should hold in light esteem? And instead of (thanking Allah for the guidance He gave you), you deny (this Message)? Then why do you not (intervene) when (the soul of a dying man) reaches its throat? And you (sit there helpless) are looking upon. But We are nearer to him than you, and you do not see it. Then why do you not, if you are exempt from account bring back the soul, if you are true (in denying this Message)? Waqia 56: 77-87

(O Mankind!) We (Allah) have certainly sent down for you a Book (Quran), in which is a message for you; will you not then understand. Anbiya 21: 10

And We (Allah) have indeed made the Quran easy to understand and remember; then is there any that will receive admonition. Qamar 54: 17

And We (Allah) sent down the Quran that which is a healing and mercy to those who believe, and it increases the wrong doers nothing but loss. Asra 17: 82

O mankind! There has come to you a good advice (Quran) from your Lord, and a healing for (all diseases of) the heart, and a guidance and mercy for the believers. Younes 10:57

All praise is due to Allah, who has sent down upon His Servant (Muhammad, PBUH), the Book (Quran), and has not placed therein any crookedness. (He has made it) clear to warn you of severe punishment from Him (to those who disbelieve), and to give glad tiding to those who believe, (and) do righteous deeds that they will have a good reward. Kahf 18: 1-2

Alif Lam Ra. This is a Book, which We (Allah) have sent down to you (O Muhammad!) so that you might bring mankind out of darkness into the light by permission of their Lord; to the path of the Exalted in Power, the Praiseworthy. Ibraheem 14: 1

And this (Quran) is a Book, which We (Allah) have revealed as a blessing, so follow it, and be righteous, that you may receive mercy. Lest you say; "the Book was only sent down to two people (Jews and Christians) before us, but we were unaware of what they studied. Or lest you say:" If the Book had been revealed to us, we should have followed its guidance better than they (Jews and Christians); So there has now come to you a clear evidence from your Lord, and a guidance and mercy (the Quran); then who could be more wrong than one who rejects the Ayaats (signs or verses) of Allah, and turns away from them? We shall recompense those who turn away from Our Ayaats (verses) with the worst of punishment for their turning away. Do they then wait fort the angels to come to them, or your Lord (Himself), or certain (more) clear signs of Your Lord? The Day that certain (such) of the signs of your Lord do come, no good will it do to a person to believe in them then, if he believed not before, nor earned good deeds through his faith, say: You wait, we too are waiting.

An'am 6: 155-157